The Official Rules
—— *for* ——
Lawyers,
Politicians...
and Everyone They Torment

**Other Official Rules Books
by Paul Dickson
Published by Walker and Company**

*The Official Rules at Home
The Official Rules at Work*

The Official Rules
for
Lawyers, Politicians...
and Everyone They Torment

Paul Dickson

Walker and Company
New York

First published in the United States of America in 1996 by
Walker Publishing Company, Inc.

Published simultaneously in Canada by Thomas Allen &
Son Canada, Limited, Markham, Ontario

Library of Congress Cataloging-in-Publication Data
The official rules for lawyers, politicians . . . and everyone
they torment/[compiled by] Paul Dickson.
p.   cm.
Includes index.
ISBN 0-8027-1321-1
1. Lawyers—United States—Humor. 2. Politicians—United
States—Humor. 3. Law—United States—Humor. 4. United
States—Politics and government—Humor.
I. Dickson, Paul.
K184.036 1996
340' .0207—dc20   96-9698
                                                      CIP

Book design by James McGuire

Printed in the United States of America

10 9 8 7 6 5 4 3 2 1

The Official Rules
_____ *for* _____

Lawyers, Politicians...

and Everyone They Torment

CALAMITAS NECESSARIA ESL

Introduction

Good times had arrived and The Murphy Center for the Codification of Human and Organizational Law was in trouble. The recession was ending, interest rates were low, a promising new president was in office, and a new tomorrow beckoned in health care. Because the Center, perverse as it is, thrives on political turmoil, bad economic times, legal buffoonery, and the widespread awareness that the universe is flawed, the future of "the world's smallest think tank" was in jeopardy.

But then, suddenly, bad news began cropping up everywhere, and things really got rolling in the summer of 1994. An obscene double-homicide on the West Coast devoured the attention of those who would let it. The recession was officially over but seemed to live on in people's heads (and wallets), a baseball strike loomed and reloomed, and health-care reform refused to loom. The right-wing blowhards who had taken over the airways went into anti-Clinton overdrive while the news media dutifully kept us posted on every twist and turn of John Bobbitt's zany post-trial life; and there were grown men in Congress who argued that the Republic would be better off if assault weapons were allowed to remain in public hands.

Then, during the second week of July 1994, somebody announced that there were only 2,000 days to go before the year 2000—the Millennium, the New Start. There was work to be done, and The Murphy Center was back in business what with all sorts of things out of whack and requiring attention.

Consider the following: In January 1995 the Postal Service raised its rates for stamps from 29¢ to 32¢ and then made it almost impossible to find 3¢ stamps to go along with the 29¢ stamps. To top it off, they issued a 29¢ commemorative that came out two days before the rate hike. In his *Fortune* column, Daniel Seligman noted, "Yours truly was among those who succeeded in buying the 3-centers and then finding that they don't stick properly when licked."

Readers of Official Rules books know that The Murphy Center for the Codification of Human and Organizational Law was founded in 1976 by yours truly, who was its first Director, and that I have been, since 1989, its self-appointed Director for Life. It was inspired by and named for Murphy's Law ("If anything can go wrong, it will") and set out to codify the truths and realities of life in imperfect times. It is housed in a growing pile of shoe boxes.

All of the observations that follow deal with politics and the law, related areas in great need of attention from The Murphy Center. They appear in the exact language of the person who discovered the law, rule, or universal truth, including his or her name for that discovery. Every attempt has been made to find the original author of each discovery, but, sadly, some appear as "unknown origin."

The items were collected over a period of years and are listed alphabetically by the name of the law, effect, or principle.

In addition to the main body of the book, The Murphy Center is proud to offer a few special bonus sections, including an official glossary of legal terms to help you understand what legal-speak is really about, as well as foolproof guides to distinguishing Republicans from Democrats and conservatives from liberals.

A

- **Abourezk's First Eight Laws of Politics.**
(1) Anybody who really would change things for
the better in this country could never be elected
president anyway. (2) Don't worry about your
enemies; it's your allies who will do you in.
(3) In politics people will do whatever is necessary to get their way. (4) The bigger the appro-
priations bill, the shorter the debate. (5) If a
politician has a choice between listening and
talking, guess which one he will choose.
(6) When voting on the confirmation of a presidential appointment, it's always safer to vote
against the son of a bitch, because if he is con-
firmed, it won't be long before he proves how
wise you were. (7) If you want to curry favor
with a politician, give him credit for something
that someone else did. (8) Don't blame me, I
voted for McGovern.

> —Former senator James
> Abourezk, from his article
> "Life Inside the
> Congressional Cookie Jar,"
> *Playboy,* March 1979

• **Acheson's Rule of the Bureaucracy.** A memorandum is written not to inform the reader but to protect the writer.
> —Former secretary of state
> Dean Acheson (1893–1971)

• **Ackley's Law.** Every recovery is hailed by an incumbent president as the result of his own wise policies, while every recession is condemned by him as the result of the mistaken policies of his predecessor.
> —Gardner Ackley, chairman
> of the Council of Economic
> Advisers under President
> Johnson; submitted by Neal
> Wilgus, Albuquerque, New
> Mexico

• **Acton's Law.** Power tends to corrupt; absolute power corrupts absolutely.
> —Lord Acton. Perhaps the
> most oft-quoted and useful of
> all political tenets.

• **Adams's Political Discovery.** Practical politics consists in ignoring facts.
> —Historian Henry Adams

• **Alice's Law.** The purpose of presidential office is not power, or leadership of the Western

World, but reminiscence, best-selling reminiscence.

> —Alice is not identified, but she was quoted by Roger Jellinek, *New York Times Book Review,* March 10, 1968.

• **Alinsky's Sword.** Favors granted always become defined as rights.

> —Saul Alinsky, 1960s community organizer; from Stu Goldstein, M.D.

• **Alsop's Law of Political Oratory.** The important thing is to be able to say "Most oranges are round" and sound as if you mean it.

> —John Alsop whose brother, columnist Joseph Alsop, directed Dwight Eisenhower's successful 1952 presidential election campaign in Connecticut and saw that Adlai Stevenson's inability to fulfill Alsop's Law may have cost him the election

• **Anderson's Distinction.** My grandfather believed there are two kinds of people: those who know how the world fits together and those who think they know. The former work in hardware stores, the latter in politics.

> —Josef Anderson, quoted in the *Los Angeles Times;* from Robert D. Specht

• **Armey's Axioms** (a selection). (1) The politics of greed always come wrapped in the language of love. (2) If you want the government to get off your back, you've got to get your hands out of its pocket. (3) You can't put your finger on a problem when you've got it to the wind. (4) It's easier (and more fun) to pass new laws than to enforce existing ones.

> —House Majority Leader Richard Armey, from his 1995 book *The Freedom Revolution*

• **Ash's Axiom.** Any request prefaced by the word "just" will be unjust (e.g., "This will just take a second," "This will just hurt for a moment," etc.).

> —Bill Ash, Miami Lakes, Florida

_B_

- **Babbitt's Evolutionary Discovery.** Evan Mecham proves that Darwin was wrong.
  > —Senator Bruce Babbitt, fomer governor of Arizona, on the then governor, quoted in _Newsweek,_ November 16, 1987

- **Baer's Quartet.** What's good politics is bad economics; what's bad politics is good economics; what's good economics is bad politics; what's bad economics is good politics.
  > —Eugene W. Baer of Middletown, Rhode Island. Baer also allows that it can all be stated somewhat more compactly as "What's good politics is bad economics and vice versa, vice versa."

- **Baker's First Law of Federal Geometry.** A block grant is a solid mass of money surrounded on all sides by governors.
  > —Ross K. Baker, _American Demographics,_ January 1982

• **Baker's Secrets of Losing Politics.**
(1) Address yourself to the issues. (2) Identify
as closely as possible with politicians. (3) Be a
loyal party person. (4) Invoke the memories of
your party greats. (5) If you are squeamish
about your partisanship, at least have the good
grace to refer to the accomplishments of your
party's major officeholders. (6) Take the high
road. (7) Never criticize your opponent's absen-
teeism on votes if you are seeking his congressional seat. (8) Never criticize your opponent
for spending too much time in the district.
(9) Avoid squandering huge amounts of money
in media markets where only a fraction of the
television audience is made up of your potential
voters. (10) Forget about the endorsements of
Hollywood celebrities and sports figures.

> —Ross K. Baker, professor of
> political science, Rutgers
> University. First revealed in
> the *New York Times,*
> December 5, 1978

• **Barnicle's Whitewater Discovery.** The
most sordid aspect of Whitewater is that all the
stuff Webster Hubbell bought from Victoria's
Secret was for Warren Christopher.

> —Mike Barnicle, *Boston
> Globe*

• **Battleson's Blatherskite.** Caveats are always* forgotten.
  * Caveat: except in rare instances.

> —Kirk Battleson, Oakton, Virginia, who adds a note of explanation: "In Washington . . . and probably everywhere else, caveats are applied to many statements. The objective may be to cover the author or speaker's 'credibility' while at the same time selling a potentially dubious project, but the hope is that the main message will be remembered and the caveat forgotten.

• **Beardsley's Warning to Lawyers.** Beware of and eschew pompous prolixity.

> —Charles A. Beardsley, the late president of the American Bar Association

• **Beck's Political Laws.** (1) A politician's gestures increase in direct proportion to the number of his media consultants. (2) Campaign expenses always rise to exceed contributions. (3) In politics, an ounce of image is worth a pound of good ideas. *Corollary:* A good slogan beats a good solution. (4) Flubs get more news coverage than facts.

> —Joan Beck, *Chicago Tribune*, January 23, 1984; from Steve Stine, Chicago, Illinois

• **Bendiner's Election Rule.** No matter how frighteningly the campaigners warn you that the salvation of the world depends on their winning, remember that on November 9, half of them will be wiring congratulations to the other half on their great victory and promising to co-operate fully in the predicted disaster.

> —Robert Bendiner, from his article "How to Listen to Campaign Oratory If You Have To," *Look*, October 11, 1960

• **Bernstein's Principle of Homogeneity.** Behavior and personality traits are relatively constant even in very different situations and relationships. *Corollary 1:* You can't be one kind of person and another kind of president.

> —Barbara Bernstein, Bowie, Maryland

• **Beste's Law Librarian's Rules.** (1) Lawyers don't read law books, they stack them. Once the stack is full enough, the research memo is written. (2) You will receive at least ten advertisements from any publisher for a book you would never, ever need to buy. (3) The attorneys most likely to bombard you with handwritten notes to buy a particular book or reporting service are partners who haven't set foot in the firm library in ten years. (4) The attorney who calls to ask you to find a "vitally important" article will never remember the title, author, or date it was published, only that he needs it by 5:00 P.M. today. (5) If you can't find a book, look for it by the copy machine. (6) The attorney who raises hell about a missing book will have at least six in his office he didn't bother checking out. (7) The books on contracts, small claims court, and do-it-yourself divorce are always missing.

—Ian R. Beste, Montrose, California

• **Bierman's Law of Contracts.** (1) In any given document, you can't cover all the "what ifs." (2) Lawyers stay in business resolving all the unresolved "what ifs." (3) Every resolved "what if" creates two unresolved "what ifs."

—Melvin Bierman, APO, Miami

• **Bismarck's Law.** The less people know about how sausages and laws are made, the better they'll sleep at night.
> —Otto Von Bismarck (1815–1898). This law seems to pop up every time a complex piece of legislation is passed.

• **Bloom's Seventh Law of Litigation.** The judge's jokes are always funny.
> —Judith Ilene Bloom, Los Angeles, California

• **Boren's Presidential Motto.** I've got what it takes to take what you've got.
> —Humorist James Boren's 1984 presidential platform

• **Broder's Warnings.** (1) Anybody that wants the presidency so much that he'll spend two years organizing and campaigning for it is not to be trusted with the office. (2) When "everybody" in the nation's capital agrees on something, it is prudent to be skeptical.
> —David Broder in his *Washington Post* columns for July 19, 1973, and May 22, 1988, respectively

• **Brooks's Catch-22s of Conservation and Renewable Energy.** (1) If savings from a proposed conservation measure are small, the measure is not considered worth the government's time; however, if savings are large, the measure is said to be too disruptive of the economy.
(2) If the measure depends on voluntary compliance, the objection is that it will not work; however, if it depends on mandatory compliance, it cannot be countenanced by the government.
(3) If the measure is cost-effective, it is asked why the government should give people money to do something they should do by themselves anyway; if it is not cost-effective, it is asked why the government should give people money to do something that will not pay off. (4) And finally, the measure can be quashed completely by declaring the matter a provincial responsibility.
> —David Brooks, former director, Office of Energy Conservation, Ottawa, Canada; from Steven Woodbury

• **Buchwald's Theorem.** Tax reform is when you take the taxes off things that have been taxed in the past and put taxes on things that haven't been taxed before.
> —Art Buchwald, quoted in *Forbes*, April 26, 1982

• **Burroughs's Projection.** The Martians are a happy people; they have no lawyers.

> —Edgar Rice Burroughs (1875–1950), novelist and creator of Tarzan

• **Bush's Discovery.** It's no exaggeration to say the undecideds could go one way or the other.

> —George Bush, discussing the 1988 campaign, quoted in *The Wit and Wisdom of George Bush;* compiled by Ken Brady and Jeremy Solomon (1989)

• **Byrd's Last Law of Politics.** Potholes know no party.

> —Senate Majority Leader Robert Byrd during the 1987 debate on the President's veto of the highway bill

C

• **Callahan's Corollary of Smith's Political Dictum.** The key to success in politics is absolute honesty. If you can fake that, you have it made.

> —From David M. Callahan, Albuquerque, New Mexico, who adds: "This has been variously attributed to Johnson, Nixon, Reagan, and Bush, as well as to Mark Russell and Johnny Carson. . . . I liked it so much, I stole it."

• **Carver's Law.** The trouble with radicals is that they read only radical literature, and the trouble with conservatives is that they don't read anything.

> —Harvard professor Thomas Nixon Carver, quoted in *New Republic,* March 28, 1970, and identified as a conservative monument of half a century ago; submitted by Joseph C. Goulden

PAUL DICKSON

- **Chaplin's Rules.** (1) The smaller the
democracy, the more complicated its political
system. (2) The newer the democracy, the
longer its national anthem.
> —Stephen M. Chaplin,
> McLean, Virginia

- **Chapman's Theorem of Justice.** The
courts are the last refuge of the unpersuasive.
> —Stephen Chapman in his
> *Chicago Tribune* column

- **Chesterton's Point.** My country right or
wrong is a thing that no patriot would think of
saying, except in a desperate case. It is like saying, "My mother, drunk or sober."
> —G. K. Chesterton, from
> Jonathan Green's *The Cynic's
> Lexicon*

- **Chuck's Law of Contract Negotiations.**
Travesty is a constant—no matter which side of
the table you sit on.
> —From Gerald Lee Steese,
> Long Beach, California, who
> heard it from a guy named
> Chuck

• **Clark's Tax Law.** When a lot of people are doing something stupid, the reason for it will be found in the tax laws.
> —George L. Clark, Sr.,
> Manhattan Beach,
> California

• **Clinton's Law of Politics.** Whenever possible, be introduced by someone you've given a good job to.
> —President Bill Clinton, after being introduced by Hillary Rodham Clinton in a speech on health care at Johns Hopkins University in October 1993

• **Clinton's Rules of Politics.** (1) Most people are for change in general, but against it in particular. (2) Never tell anyone to go to hell unless you can make 'em go. (3) Whenever someone tells you, "It's nothing personal," he's about to stick it to you. (4) Whenever it is possible for a person to shift the heat from himself to the governor, he'll do it. (5) Under enough pressure, most people—but not everybody—will stretch the truth on you. (6) You're most vulnerable in politics when you think you're the least vulnerable. (7) When you start enjoying something, it's probably time to leave. (8) Never look

past the next election; it might be your last.
(9) There's no such thing as enough money.
(10) Don't drink in public. You might act like
yourself.

> —Governor Bill Clinton,
> quoted in *On the Make: The
> Rise of Bill Clinton* by
> Meredith L. Oakley; from the
> late Charles D. Poe

• **Cohen's Political Laws.** *Law of
Candidates:* Many people run for office only
because someone they know and don't like is
running for the same office. *Law of Political
Polling:* Sometimes those who lead in the pub-
lic-opinion polls win the election. *Law of
Recollections:* Recollections of personal animosi-
ties generally last longer than the recollections
of the effects of public policies. *Law of
Alienation:* Nothing can so alienate a voter from
the political system as backing a winning candidate. *Law of Attraction:* Power attracts people,
but it cannot hold them. *Law of Competition:*
The more qualified candidates who are available, the more likely the compromise will be on
the candidate whose main qualification is a
nonthreatening incompetence. *Law of Inside
Dope:* There are many inside dopes in politics
and government. *Law on Lawmaking:* Those
who express random thoughts to legislative

committees are often surprised and appalled to find themselves the instigators of law. *Law of Permanence:* Political power is as permanent as today's newspaper. Ten years from now, few will know or care who the most powerful man in any state was today. *Law of Secrecy:* The best way to publicize a governmental or political action is to attempt to hide it. *Law of Wealth:* Victory goes to the candidate with the most accumulated or contributed wealth who has the financial sources to convince the middle class and poor that he will be on their side. *Law of Wisdom:* Wisdom is considered a sign of weakness by the powerful because a wise man can lead without power but only a powerful man can lead without wisdom.

> —Mark B. Cohen, while a
> member of the House of
> Representatives, Common-
> wealth of Pennsylvania

• **Congress, Universal Law of.** Neither the House nor the Senate shall pass a law they shall be subject to.

> —Unknown origin, collected
> on a radio call-in show. The
> truth of this law is much
> proven, as Congress has
> exempted itself from such
> laws as the Civil Rights Act of

1964, the Equal Pay Act, the
Privacy Act of 1974,
Americans with Disabilities
Act of 1990, and—stand
back—the Ethics in
Government Act of 1978

• **Conner's Rewrite.** For every wrong, there
is a lawyer willing to take it on contingency.
—Edmond M. Conner, a
Southern California lawyer
quoted in the *Los Angeles
Times*. This is a reworking of
the maxim of jurisprudence
that holds: "For every wrong
there is a remedy."

• **The Cook County Immutable Law of
Politics.** Once a vote has been stolen, it stays
stolen.
—Traditional tenet of
Chicago politics

• **Corvin's Rule of Rules.** If you screw the
rules, they will multiply.
—G. F. Corvin, Nairobi,
Kenya

• **Cotton's Explanation.** One can usually tell
from the degree of formality with which one

senator refers to another what the nature of their personal relations may be. If the reference is made casually as "Senator Jones," they are probably close friends. If someone refers to a colleague as "the Senator from Michigan," one may infer that they have a cordial relationship. If a senator refers to another as "the distinguished Senator from Indiana," one may assume he does not particularly like him. And if he refers to him as the "very able and distinguished Senator from California," it usually indicates that he hates his guts.

> —Senator Norris Cotton,
> from his book *In the Senate,*
> Dodd, Mead, 1978

• **Cradock's First Law of Diplomacy.** It is not the other side you need to worry about, but your own.

> —British diplomat Sir Percy
> Cradock, from his 1994 book
> *Experiences of China*

• **Crenna's Discovery.** Futurism is passé. *Crenna's Law of Political Accountability:* If you are the first to know about something bad, you are going to be held responsible for acting on it, regardless of your formal duties.

> —Policy adviser C. D.
> Crenna, Ottawa, Canada

• **Cruickshank's Law of Government.** We have met the enemy. In fact, we elected him.

> —Ken Cruickshank, *Florida Times-Union*, (Jacksonville), from his June 25, 1978, column

• **Curley's Political Laws.** (1) As long as they spell the name right. (2) Every time you do a favor for a constituent, you make nine enemies and one ingrate.

> —Lines uttered by the famous Boston mayor, Massachusetts governor, and U.S. congressman James Michael Curley, whose legendary response to bad publicity was to shrug his shoulders and insist that he did not mind as long as they got his name right

D

• **Dabney's Prime Axiom of Washington Thought.** Ideas are rarely the weapons of political struggle. *Corollaries:* (1) There is no such thing as truth. (2) Anyone who deals in general ideas is merely pushing the interests of his class, or of whoever's paying. (3) There is no such thing as right and wrong. (4) No one is capable of speaking to the general good.

> —Dick Dabney, *Washington Post,* October 16, 1979

• **Dart's Dictum.** Talking to politicians is fine, but with a little money they hear you better.

> —Justin Dart, chairman, Dart Industries, quoted by Mark Green in *New Republic,* December 13, 1982

• **Davidson's Maxim.** Democracy is that form of government where everybody gets what the majority deserves.

> —James Dale Davidson, executive director of the National Taxpayers' Union

• **Davis's Warning.** Always be suspicious of a politician who says that something can never happen.

> —Dr. M. I. M. Davis, Surrey, England

• **Dean's Law of the District of Columbia.** Washington is a much better place if you are asking questions rather than answering them.

> —John Dean, former counsel to President Nixon, on the occasion of beginning his syndicated radio interview show

• **DeRoy's Political Rule.** A politician solves every problem before election but very few after.

> —Richard H. DeRoy, Hilo, Hawaii

• **Dershowitz's Apologia for Ambulance Chasers.** It's not a chase, it's a race. The good ambulance chasers are always in a race against the claims adjusters.

> —Attorney and professor Alan Dershowitz, as quoted in the *Boston Globe;* from Bob Skole

• **Dickens's Discovery on Justice.** If there were no bad people, there would be no good lawyers.

—Charles Dickens

• **Dirksen's Three Laws of Politics.** (1) Get elected. (2) Get reelected. (3) Don't get mad, get even.

—Senator Everett Dirksen,
recalled by Harry N. D.
Fisher; from Alan L. Otten

• **Dole's Razor.** Public television viewers are "affluent, highly educated, the movers and shakers, the socially conscious and the well informed." What about the rest of us?

—Senator Bob Dole, June 3,
1992, citing a description of
public television's audience
while opposing a bill for public broadcasting

• **Drake's Disaster Dictum.** There are two things that don't work when disaster strikes: God and government.

—Dorothy Drake,
Birmingham Post-Herald,
September 18, 1992; from
Grady Nunn

• **DuBow's Laws of Attorney Fee Compensation.** (1) Never accept a check from a man accused of passing bad ones. (2) Never accept cash from a man accused of counterfeiting.

> —Myron DuBow, Sherman Oaks, California

• **Dugger's Law of Texas Politics.** Possession is the first nine-tenths of the law, and politics is the tenth.

> —Ronnie Dugger, in *The Politician;* from Joseph C. Goulden

• **du Pont's Laws.** A COMPENDIUM OF HELPFUL RULES GOVERNING THE LEGISLATIVE PROCESS NOT TO BE FOUND IN JEFFERSON'S MANUAL OF RULES AND PRACTICES OF THE HOUSE OF REPRESENTATIVES. (1) Vote as an individual; lemmings end up falling off cliffs. (2) The speed at which the legislative process seems to work is in inverse proportion to your enthusiasm for the bill. (3) The titles of bills—like those of Marx Brothers movies—often have little to do with the substance of the legislation. Particularly deceptive are bills containing title buzzwords such as "emergency," "reform," "service," "relief," or "special." Often the "emergency" is of the writer's imagination; the "reform," a protection of vested interest; the

"service," self-serving; the "relief," an additional
burden on the taxpayer; and the "special," something that otherwise shouldn't be passed.
(4) Sometimes the best law of all is no law at all.
Not all the world's ills are susceptible to legislative correction. (5) When voting on appropria-
tions bills, more is not necessarily better. It is
as wasteful to have a B-1 bomber in every
garage as it is to have a welfare program for
every conceivable form of deprivation. (6) The
Crusades ended several centuries ago after
killing thousands of people. The most important issues arouse intense passions. Earmuffs to
block the shouting are inappropriate, but filter
the feedback. Joining a cause and leading a
constituency are not mutually exclusive, but neither are they necessarily synonymous. Neither
welfare nor profits are "obscene." (7) "Beware
the [lobbyist], my son, the jaws that bite, the
claws that snatch" (with thanks to Lewis
Carroll). No matter how noble the cause or
well-meaning its professional advocates, lobbyists are still paid to get results. They're subject
to errors in judgment, shortcomings in motives,
and most of them don't even vote in your district. (8) Mirror, mirror on the wall, who's the
fairest one of all? The press is hopelessly biased
or genuinely fair, depending upon whose views
are being misquoted, misrepresented, or misun-
derstood. (9) If you are concerned about being

criticized—you're in the wrong job. However
you vote, and whatever you do, somebody will
be out there telling you that you are: (a) wrong,
(b) insensitive, (c) a bleeding heart, (d) a pawn
of somebody else, (e) too wishy-washy, (f) too
unwilling to compromise, (g) all of the above—
consistency is not required of critics.

—Former governor Pierre S.
du Pont of Delaware, who
wrote them when he was a
congressman. The laws were
written for incoming mem-
bers, about whom he said in
his introduction to the laws:
"A freshman Congressman
trying to do his job properly
is similar to a quarterback
trying to throw a 60-yard
pass with a deflated football.
The only difference is the
quarterback knows there is
no air in the ball—the freshman Congressman doesn't
even know what game he is
playing."

E

• **Emery's Law.** Regulation is the substitution of error for chance.
> —Fred J. Emery, director,
> *Federal Register*, Washington,
> D.C.

• **Enthoven's Discovery.** The ideal weapons system is built in 435 congressional districts, and it doesn't matter whether it works or not.
> —Stanford economist and
> former Pentagon official
> Alain C. Enthoven, quoted in
> the *Washington Post*, January
> 26, 1992; from Joseph C.
> Goulden

• **Evans's Law of Political Perfidy.** When our friends get into power, they aren't our friends anymore.
> —M. Stanton Evans, former
> head of the American
> Conservative Union

F

• **Faber's Law.** If there isn't a law, there will be.

> —Harold Faber in a 1968
> *New York Times Magazine*
> article on laws, principles,
> axioms, and the like

• **Fannie's Gonif Theory.** (1) Most politicians are thieves. (2) Most politicians are slow learners. (3) Therefore, never vote for an incumbent. While the challenger's natural inclinations are equally bad, it will take him time to learn how to achieve his goals.

> —From Carl T. Bogus,
> Philadelphia, Pennsylvania,
> who attributes it to his aunt
> Fannie, Mrs. Fagel Kanev.
> *Gonif* is Yiddish for thief.

• **First Law of Holes.** When in one, stop digging.

> —Oft-quoted law of unknown
> origin applied in many situa-
> tions. For instance, William

Safire invoked it in 1992
when George Bush insisted
that he had no knowledge of
Saddam Hussein's abuse of
U.S. grain credits to buy
destructive technology.

• **Fitzwater's Prescription for Improving the Clinton White House.** A few more fat old bald men wouldn't hurt the place.

—Former Bush administration press secretary Marlin Fitzwater, quoted in *Newsweek*, June 7, 1993

• **Flak Diversion Theorem.** A published remark by any congressman that irritates a lobbying association or the White House is automatically labeled by his office as "taken out of context."

—*Washington Star*, unsigned editorial, February 18, 1979

• **Flory's Law.** Whenever you put out a trough full of public money, you are going to find some pigs with all four feet in it.

—K. C. Flory, Oconomowoc, Wisconsin

• **Foley's Rules for Politicians.** (1) Don't go to spelling bees. (2) Don't shoot muzzle-loading rifles at targets. (3) Don't throw a baseball unless you have a very high box to drop it from . . . straight down. Do not go out on the mound and try to toss it across the field. (4) Don't wear hats, that sort of thing. (5) Don't ride horses at rodeos. Don't even ride them in parades. (6) Never ride in a Rolls Royce.
> —Former House Speaker Tom Foley to a group of reporters on June 22, 1992, reacting to Dan Quayle's problem spelling potato(e) at a spelling bee

• **France's Law of Law.** The law, in its majestic equality, forbids the rich as well as the poor to sleep under bridges, to beg in the streets, and to steal bread.
> —Author Anatole France (1844–1924)

• **Frankel's Law.** Whatever happens in government could have happened differently, and it usually would have been better if it had. *Corollary:* Once things have happened, no matter how accidentally, they will be regarded as manifestations of an unchangeable Higher Reason.

—Professor Charles Frankel of Columbia University, from his book, *High on Foggy Bottom,* Harper & Row, 1969

• **Fresco's Query.** Why is it when liberals win elections it is called polarization, yet when conservatives are victorious it is labeled a mandate?

—Victor Fresco, letter to the *Los Angeles Times,* June 25, 1981; from Robert D. Specht

• **Freund's Advice.** Be concise for clients. Less is more. Bravura displays only serve to irritate; brevity is what pays the rent.

—James C. Freund, quoted in *Leadership* by William Safire and Leonard Safir

G

- **Galbraith's Law of Political Wisdom.** Anyone who says he isn't going to resign, four times, definitely will.
                    —John Kenneth Galbraith

- **Giffin's Paradox.** If it weren't for lawyers, we wouldn't need them.
                    —A. K. Giffin, Dorval,
                    Quebec, Canada

- **Gillers's Equation.** The richer you are, the more justice you get.
                    —Stephen Gillers, New York
                    University law professor,
                    commenting in 1994 on O. J.
                    Simpson's all-star defense
                    team

- **Gilmer's Law of Political Leadership.** Look over your shoulder now and then to be sure someone's following you.
                    —Uttered by Virginia's state
                    treasurer Henry Gilmer some

thirty years ago and recently
quoted in a syndicated column by James J. Kilpatrick

• **Gilmore's Warning.** The worse the society,
the more law there will be. In Hell there will be
nothing but law, and due process will be meticu-
lously observed.

> —Grant Gilmore in the *New
> York Times,* February 23,
> 1977; from Don Nilsen

• **The Glover-Baxendale Warning.** Never
step between a young lawyer and a moving
ambulance.

> —Boykin A. Glover,
> Alexandria, Virginia, and
> Hadley V. Baxendale,
> Baltimore, Maryland, who
> individually came up with
> this warning in response to a
> 1979 "National Challenge"
> contest to come up with a
> modern maxim. Submitted
> by J. Baxter Newgate, who
> ran the "National Challenge."

• **Gold's Law.** The candidate who is expected
to do well because of experience and reputation
(Douglas, Nixon) must do *better* than well, while

the candidate expected to fare poorly (Lincoln, Kennedy) can put points on the media board simply by surviving.

> —Vic Gold, in *P.R. as in President,* Doubleday, 1977

• **Goldwyn's Law of Contracts.** A verbal contract isn't worth the paper it's written on.

> —Samuel Goldwyn

• **Goulden's Law of Jury Watching.** If a jury in a criminal trial stays out for more than twenty-four hours, it is certain to vote acquittal, save in those instances where it votes guilty.

> —Joseph C. Goulden, writer, who developed the law during twenty-seven months of intensive research as a courts reporter for the *Dallas News*

• **Governor's Rule.** Everyone at the executive end of Pennsylvania Avenue considers everyone at the congressional end an s.o.b. and vice versa. The governors consider anyone from Washington an s.o.b. no matter which end of the avenue he comes from.

> —Discovered by the late Theodore C. Achilles when representing the executive branch at the Governors'

Conference in Colorado
Springs, 1949

• **Greenfield's Observations.** (1) *Democratic Rule:* Too many liberal Democrats have come, over the years, to worship . . . the state and to see it as the natural agent of the Lord's will, even though you can't reach it by telephone much after 4:30 in the afternoon. (2) *Practical Politics:* Everybody is for democracy—in principle. It's only in practice that the thing gives rise to stiff objections.

> —Meg Greenfield, *Newsweek,* December 15, 1980, from Robert Specht, and from the *Washington Post,* in a column titled "The People's Revenge," June 14, 1978, respectively

• **Guppy Law.** When outrageous expenditures are divided finely enough, the public will not have enough stake in any one expenditure to squelch it.

> —Fred Reed, columnist for the *Federal Times,* explaining how the bureaucracy minimizes popular resistance to whale-like programs by turning them into schools of tiny fish; from Alan L. Otten

H

- **Halberstam's Law of Survival.** Always stay in with the outs.
> —David Halberstam

- **Hall's Laws of Politics.** (1) The voters always want less taxes and more spending. (2) Citizens want honest politicians until they want something fixed. (3) Constituency drives out consistency (i.e., liberals defend military spending and conservatives social spending in their own districts).
> —Robert A. Hall, Minority Whip, Massachusetts senate

- **Hegel's Rules of Debate.** (1) Before you argue or debate, define the terms. (2) Before that, define "define."
> —Gene Hegel, Elgin, Illinois

- **Herburger's Law of Small-Town Lawyers.** Where there is only one lawyer in town, the lawyer can't make a living. But when there are two lawyers in town, both of them will make a good living.

—From Calvin E. Deonier,
Ritter, Oregon, who collected
it from a person named
Herburger

• **Herold's Constant.** When a politician, particularly on the stump, says that he'll "reconsider," "reevaluate," or "study" something once elected, he's going to kill it.
—R. A. Herold, Ottawa,
Ontario, Canada

• **Hewett's Observation.** The rudeness of a bureaucrat is inversely proportional to his or her position in the governmental hierarchy and to the number of peers similarly engaged (if there is one window open, it will be staffed by Godzilla's cousin).
—Paul C. Hewett, Wilmette,
Illinois

• **Honig's Discovery.** Getting your ducks in a row results in a row of duck shit.
—Dr. James Honig,
Rockledge, Florida

I

• **Ingre's Statements of Political Integrity.**
(1) To proclaim "I am against that" often means
"I would not want others to think me in favor of
it." (2) The sincerity of one's avowals is usually
tempered by a desire to win the approbation of
one's fellows.

—M. David Ingre, Ottawa,
Ontario, Canada

J

• **Jacquin's Postulate on Democratic Governments.** No man's life, liberty, or property are safe while the legislature is in session.

> —Unknown origin, unknown author

• **Johnson's Law.** Space expands to house the people to perform the work that Congress creates.

> —Writer Haynes Johnson, *Washington Post*, August 14, 1977

K

• **Kelleher's Explanation.** The Congress is constitutionally empowered to launch programs the scope, impact, consequences, and workability of which are largely unknown, at least to the Congress, at the time of enactment. The federal bureaucracy is legally permitted to execute the congressional mandate with a high degree of befuddlement as long as it acts no more befuddled than the Congress must reasonably have anticipated.

> —U.S. District Court Judge Robert Kelleher, Central District, California, in ruling on *American Petroleum Institute v. Knecht,* August 31, 1978; submitted by Steven R. Woodbury

• **Kelly's Counsel on Hiring Counsel.** On any given day, 50 percent of the lawyers in American courtrooms are losers.

> —Thomas W. Kelly, Washington, D.C.

• **Kennedy's Judgment.** Generally speaking, a lawyer who becomes a judge believes the explanation is that God noticed his work, saw that it was good, and rewarded him. This is almost never true, but if you are a trial lawyer, it is a bad idea to suggest to a judge that it is false.

> —The character Jeremiah Kennedy from George V. Higgins's 1992 book *Defending Billy Ryan;* spotted by Bob Skole

• **Kenny's Law.** There is a critical mass of lawyers in any transaction (the number being different for every transaction), which if exceeded the deal will become undoable.

> —Attorney Robert Kenny, Lawrenceville, New Jersey

• **Kenworthy's Laws of the Bureaucracy.** *Competency:* The competency of any executive-level official of government is inversely proportional to the number of his/her "special" or "executive" assistants. *Assistants:* The arrogance of any "special" or "executive" assistant to a secretarial-level official is inversely proportional to the age and experience thereof. *Career Bureaucrats:* The influence of any Government Service Career bureaucrat is inversely proportional to the age of the furnishings of his/her office. *Values in the Bureaucracy:* (1) In government, influence is most admired, longevity is most respected, but anonymity is most prized. (2) Respect is what is earned from one's supervisors instead of a promotion or raise. (3) The deeper the carpet you're called upon, the deeper the trouble you're in. *Cabinet Law:* A cabinet officer's most efficient activity is foreign travel; his/her most useful activity is domestic travel; time spent in the office is merely the necessary connection between the two. *External Relations:* (1) A lobbyist is paid to look like he's telling the truth when he's lying; a department's congressional liaison is paid to look like he's telling the truth when he really has nothing to say. (2) A reporter's brother-in-law who works for the government is known as an "informed source" when he's sober and a "leak" when he's drunk.

—Jim Kenworthy, Kansas
City, Missouri

• **Keynes's Razor.** If you owe your bank a hundred pounds, you have a problem; but if you owe a million, it has.

—John Maynard Keynes,
quoted in *The Economist,*
February 13, 1982

• **Kilpatrick's Reminder.** We have surrendered the silly notion that politicians should be above politics.

> —James J. Kilpatrick; from
> S. G. Finefrock, Chicago,
> Illinois

• **Kissinger's Discovery.** The nice thing about being a celebrity is that when you bore people, they think it's their fault.

> —Henry Kissinger, quoted by
> Bob Swift in the *Miami
> Herald*, January 3, 1987

• **Kitman's Canons of TV Law.** (1) The man on trial is never guilty. (2) The guilty person is in the court. (3) A lawyer whose name is in the title of the show never loses a case.

> —Marvin Kitman, who
> studied for the TV bar by
> watching "Perry Mason," in
> the Long Island *Newsday*
> magazine, May 25, 1986

• **Knowles's Laws.** *Bumper Stickers:* The bumper sticker always stays on longer when the candidate wins. *Legislative Deliberation:* The length of debate varies inversely with the complexity of the issue. *Corollary:* When the issue is simple, and everyone understands it, debate is almost interminable.

> —Robert P. Knowles, New Richmond, Wisconsin (see also *McFadin's Rule of Political Intelligence)*

• **Korologos's Laws.** (1) The length of your answer in a public hearing has a direct and inverse ratio to the truth. (2) The closer you get to congressional recesses, the better good government you get. (3) Congresses do two things best: nothing and overreact. (4) When fifty-one senators tell you they'll be with you if needed, you've got a problem. (5) "Thank God! They killed the prayer amendment."

> —Tom C. Korologos, Great Falls, Virginia

• **Krauthammer's Law of Indignation.** Even in Washington the capacity for waxing indignant is not infinite.

> —Charles Krauthammer, *Washington Post,* December 26, 1986

L

- **Ladof's Law of Legal Services.** A client with a bagful of papers is trouble. Ditto for briefcases or any other containers.
  > —Attorney Anne Ladof,
  > Emigsville, Pennsylvania

- **Lament for Public Defenders.** It's harder when they're really innocent.
  > —Origin unknown

- **Landon's Law of Politics.** It's a sin in politics to land a soft punch.
  > —Presidential candidate Alf
  > Landon, in an interview with
  > David Broder, *Washington
  > Post*, December 14, 1977

- **Lawyer's Rule.** When the law is against you, argue the facts. When the facts are against you, argue the law. When both are against you, call the other lawyer names.
  > —Widely quoted, but of
  > unknown origin. There are
  > many versions of it, including

this one from Judge Joe
Baldwin quoted in William
Safire and Leonard Safir's
Good Advice: "If you have a
strong case in law, talk to the
judge. If you have a strong
case in fact, talk to the jury.
But if you have no case in
law or fact, talk to the wild
elements and bellow like a
bull."

• **Legal Proverbs from Around the World.**
•Lawyers and painters can soon change black to
white (Danish). • If the laws could speak, they
would first complain of lawyers (American). •A
lean compromise is better than a fat lawsuit
(English). •Fear not the law but the judge
(American). •Laws, like the spider's web, catch
the fly and let the hawk go free (Spanish). •He
that goes to law holds a wolf by the tail
(English). •A countryman between two lawyers
is like a fish between two cats (Spanish).
•Three Philadelphia lawyers are a match for the
devil (American). •Going to law is losing a cow
for the sake of a cat (Chinese). •He that is his
own lawyer has a fool for a client (American).
•Lawyers and soldiers are the devil's playmates
(German). •A lawyer's opinion is worth nothing
unless paid for (American). •A good lawyer is a

bad neighbor (American). •The houses of
lawyers are roofed with the skins of litigants
(Welsh).
—Many sources

• **Levy's Ten Laws of the Disillusionment of
the True Liberal.** (1) Large numbers of things
are determined, and therefore not subject to
change. (2) Anticipated events never live up to
expectations. (3) That segment of the community with which one has the greatest sympathy as
a liberal inevitably turns out to be one of the
most narrow-minded and bigoted segments of
the community. (4) Always pray that your opposition be wicked. In wickedness there is a
strong strain toward rationality. Therefore there
is always the possibility, in theory, of handling
the wicked by outthinking them. *Corollary 1:*
Good intentions randomize behavior.
Subcorollary 1: Good intentions are far more dif-
ficult to cope with than malicious behavior.
Corollary 2: If good intentions are combined
with stupidity, it is impossible to outthink them.
Corollary 3: Any discovery is more likely to be
exploited by the wicked than applied by the vir-
tuous. (5) In unanimity there is cowardice and
uncritical thinking. (6) To have a sense of
humor is to be a tragic figure. (7) To know thy-
self is the ultimate form of aggression. (8) No
amount of genius can overcome a preoccupa-

tion with detail. (9) Only God can make a random selection. (10) Eternal boredom is the price of constant vigilance.

> —Marion J. Levy, Jr., chairman of the East Asian studies department, Princeton University

• **Lief's Law.** There's always plenty of free cheese in a mousetrap.

> —Greg Lief, Arlington, Virginia; from Tom Gill, Lubbock, Texas, with wide application, but especially relevant to politics

• **Lippmann's Political Rule.** [A] democratic politician had better not be right too soon. Very often the penalty is political death. It is much safer to keep in step with the parade of opinion than to try to keep up with the swifter movement of events.

> —Walter Lippmann, in *The Public Philosophy*, New American Library

• **Littlejohn's Lament.** I don't think there are very many lawyers who don't stare out the window and dream of doing something else.

> —James Littlejohn, lawyer,

Estes Park, Colorado, quoted
in the August 10, 1984, *USA
Today*

• **Lloyd George's Razor.** A politician is a
person with whose politics you don't agree; if
you agree with him he is a statesman.
—British statesman David
Lloyd George (1863–1945)

M

• **Macaulay's Reality Check.** To make our-selves feel good and democratic, we say a lawyer is a lawyer is a lawyer, but the only time these people come together is in the Yellow Pages.
>—Stewart Macaulay,
>University of Wisconsin,
>quoted in *USA Today*, August
>10, 1984

• **Maddocks's Law of Thermopolitical Dynamics.** If a less powerful person or group makes things hot for a more powerful person or group, that person or group is likely to make things an awful lot hotter for junior.
>—Melvin Maddocks from a
>*Christian Science Monitor*
>article on whistle-blowers;
>from Steven R. Woodbury

• **Mankiewicz's Laws.** *Second Law of Politics:* A politician will always tip off his true belief by stating the opposite at the beginning of the sentence. For maximum comprehension, do not start listening until the first clause is concluded. Begin instead at the word "but," which begins the second—or active—clause. This is the way to tell a liberal from a conservative—before they tell you. Thus: "I have always believed in a strong national defense, second to none, but . . ." (a liberal, about to propose a $20 billion cut in the defense budget).

> —Frank Mankiewicz, former president of National Public Radio and former press secretary to the 1972 McGovern campaign. The *Second Law of Politics* originally appeared in the *Washingtonian*, July 1975. As for his *First Law of Politics,* he explains, "All of my laws of politics are 'second' on the theory that I will find a better one."

• **Mann's Proposition.** Any politician who perceives the problem insists upon full credit for its solution.

> —Robert T. Mann, chairman, Florida Public Service Commission; from D. Franklin Skinner, Miami, Florida

• **The Marshall Cook Theory.** Jurors will give up the casual clothing they've been wearing for coats, ties, and formal dresses on the day their verdict is ready.

> —Named for a U.S. marshal
> in the court of Judge Aubrey
> E. Robinson, Jr., and reported
> in the *Washington Times* by
> Jay Mallin, July 11, 1986;
> from Joseph C. Goulden

• **Marshall's Memorandum to Vice-Presidential Aspirants.** There were two brothers: One ran away to sea, and the other was elected to vice president—and nothing was ever heard from either of them again.

> —Vice President Thomas R.
> Marshall, who is best recalled
> for his immortal prescription
> for the nation: "What this
> country needs is a good five-
> cent cigar."

• **Maverick's Observation.** You can fool some of the people all of the time and all of the people some of the time—and them's pretty good odds.

> —The old "Maverick" TV
> show; from Don Coles, St.
> Louis, Missouri

• **McAdoo's Maxims.** *Rule of Political Self-Interest:* Whenever a beneficial measure is opposed by powerful financial interests, the real reason for the opposition is never given. *Political Mendacity:* (1) Make the lie highly personal, for lies about a party or a class are too cold and abstract to arouse more than a faint public interest. (2) Create and disseminate a vague story, rather than one which hangs on precise data. The more vague and foggy it is the better, as it is likely to live longer than a detailed lie, which can be disputed by facts. . . . Vagueness leaves a great deal to the imagination, and people are likely to imagine the worst. . . . All you have to do is to launch the lie in general terms, and the public will supply the details, so that the story grows by much retelling.

> —William G. McAdoo, secretary of the treasury under Woodrow Wilson, in *The Crowded Years;* from Joseph C. Goulden

• **McCarthy's Law of Intelligence.** Being in politics is like being a football coach. You have to be smart enough to understand the game and dumb enough to think it's important.

> —Widely quoted law from former senator and presidential candidate Eugene McCarthy

• **McCarthy's Warnings.** (1) It is dangerous for a national candidate to say things that people might remember. (2) Remember that the worst accidents occur in the middle of the road. (3) (To new members of Congress) Vote against anything introduced with a "re" in it, especially reforms, reorganizations, and recodifications. This usually means going back to something that failed once and is likely to do so again.

> —Eugene McCarthy, quoted in the *Washington Post,* September 4, 1984, and his article "Ten Commandments for New Hill Members," *Washington Post,* January 4, 1981

• **McClaughry's Laws.** *Public Policy:* Politicians who vote huge expenditures to alleviate problems get reelected; those who propose structural changes to prevent problems get early retirement. *Reform:* Liberals, but not conservatives, can get attention and acclaim for denouncing liberal policies that failed; and liberals will inevitably capture the ensuing agenda for "reform." *Iron Law of Zoning:* When it's not needed, zoning works fine; when it is essential, it always breaks down.

> —John McClaughry, Concord, Vermont. The last law was

born when McClaughry was studying the effects of zoning in the course of the 1974 debate on the Vermont Land Use Plan. As he explains, "A speaker had urged state zoning to 'keep Vermont from turning into Los Angeles.' When it was pointed out that Los Angeles had had zoning in force since 1923, McClaughry's Iron Law rapidly emerged. I was at the time chairman of the Planning Commission of Kirby, Vermont, population 230, which had zoning but absolutely no need for it since there was no development pressure."

• **McFadin's Rule of Political Intelligence.** The smart man puts his bumper stickers on the morning after the election.
—Bill McFadin, Jacksonville, Florida (see **Knowles's Laws**)

• **McGlinchey's Law of Trust.** Never trust a world leader.

> —Herbert J. McGlinchey, former U.S. congressman, Pennsylvania state senator, and Philadelphia ward leader

• **Miles's Political Prayer.** Yea, even though I graze in pastures with jackasses, I pray that I will not bray like one.

> —William Miles, Anna Marie, Florida

• **Mills's Law.** The bigger the problem, the fewer the facts.

> —Harlan D. Mills in *Mathematics and the Managerial Imagination;* from Mel Loftus

•**Mitchell's Rule of the Reign.** Get rid of anybody who yammers daily about salvation, the sacredness of the family, and the honor of the republic, because it amuses people too much when the truth comes out.

> —The late Henry Mitchell in his *Washington Post* article January 23, 1981, based on a lifetime of observing politicians fall from grace

- **Mollick's Value of the Vindictive Voter** (a.k.a. Mollick's Measure of the Malevolent Majority). In a democratic election, the majority invariably votes against the loser and not for the winner.
  —John J. Mollick, Bowie, Maryland

- **Montero's Principle.** An attorney who informs the judge that he has "just one more question" will, invariably, keep the witness on the stand an additional half hour to forty-five minutes. However, if he informed the judge that he has "just several more questions," then the witness will be on the stand for several days.
  —Wilson M. Montero, Jr., New Orleans, Louisiana

- **Moriarty's Laws.** (1) Those who think that there is nothing new under the sun have never practiced law. (2) Your ability to pick up errors improves with each succeeding draft of a document. (3) Time does not bring experience. Time just makes you old.
  —Attorney James P. Moriarty, Presque Isle, Maine

• **Mosher's Law.** It's better to retire too soon than too late.

> —Representative Charles A. Mosher (R-Ohio), on retiring at age seventy after sixteen years in Congress

• **Moyers's Discovery.** The worst thing you can do to the liberals is to deprive them of their grievances.

> —Commentator Bill Moyers, at the Democratic National Convention, August 13, 1980; from Robert D. Specht

• **Moynihan's Architectural Solution.** Whereas in the fall of 1980 the frame of the New Senate Office Building was covered with plastic sheathing in order that construction might continue during the winter months; and

Whereas the plastic cover has not been removed revealing, as feared, a building whose banality is exceeded only by its expense; and

Whereas even in a democracy there are things it is as well the people do not know about their government: Now, therefore, be it

Resolved, that it is the sense of the Senate that the plastic cover be put back.

> —New York Senator Daniel P.
> Moynihan, text of Senate
> Resolution #140, May 19,
> 1981

• **Murphy's Discovery.** Presidents talk to the country the way men talk to women: "Trust me, go all the way with me, and everything will be all right." And what happens? Nine months later you're in trouble!

> —Maureen Murphy, on TV's
> "The Tonight Show"; from
> Robert D. Specht

• **Murray's Analogy.** Law sufficiently complex is indistinguishable from no law at all.

> —Charles Murray, *National
> Review,* June 10, 1988; from
> the late Charles D. Poe

• **Murray's Rule.** Any country with "democratic" in the title isn't.

> —Columnist Jim Murray, *Los
> Angeles Times,* August 3,
> 1980; from Robert D. Specht

• **Muskie's Rule.** Only talk when it improves the silence.

> —The late Senator Edmund S. Muskie, whose strategy to get what he wanted as head of the Senate Budget Committee was to let everyone else get talked out; reported by Steve Campbell in the *Maine Sunday Telegram*, August 4, 1991

N

- **Naden's Law.** Any idea held by a person that was not put in by reason, cannot be taken out by reason.

  —Kenneth D. Naden,
  Bethesda, Maryland

- **Naiman's Rules of Politics.** (1) The only way to have a candidate who agrees with you on every issue is to run yourself. (2) An officeholder will be worse than his predecessor but better than his successor.

  —Joe Naiman, San Diego,
  California

- **Niebuhr's Law of the Jungle.** Everyone out there is someone else's lunch.

  —Mike Niebuhr, Dallas, Texas

- **Noble's Law of Political Imagery.** All other things being equal, a bald man cannot be elected President of the United States.
  Corollary: Given a choice between two bald

political candidates, the American people will
vote for the less bald of the two.

>—Bald writer Vic Gold in his
>*Washingtonian* article "Can a
>Bald Man Be Elected
>President?" Noble is G.
>Vance Noble, author of *The
>Hirsute Tradition in American
>Politics,* widely believed to be
>one of Gold's alter egos

• **Nofziger's Law of Details.** The American
people aren't interested in details.

>—Lyn Nofziger, when he was
>on Ronald Reagan's presiden-
>tial campaign staff, comment-
>ing on the tendency of politi-
>cians to give analysis on such
>things as the comparative
>defense capabilities of two
>prototype aircraft. From Vic
>Gold's *P.R. as in President* (see
>***Spencer's [Contradictory]
>Corollary***)

• **Nolan's Law.** If you outsmart your lawyer,
you've got the wrong lawyer.

>—Attorney John T. Nolan,
>Iowa City, Iowa

• **Nyhan's Law.** You never have more friends than the day before you announce a run for president.

> —David Nyhan in his *Boston Globe* column of November 3, 1995

O

• Oaks's Unruly Laws for Lawmakers.
(1) Law expands in proportion to the resources available for its enforcement. *Corollaries to the First Law:* (a) The public is easily fooled by government claims of economizing. (b) A uninformed lawmaker is more likely to produce a complicated law than a simple one. (c) Bad or complicated law tends to drive out good judgment. (2) Bad law is more likely to be supplemented than repealed. (3) Social legislation cannot repeal physical laws.

> —Dallin H. Oaks, president of Brigham Young University. The laws first appeared in his essay "Unruly Laws for Lawmakers," in the *Congressional Record* for March 17, 1978

• O'Brien's First Law of Politics.
The more campaigning, the better.

> —Larry O'Brien, during the time he was running John F. Kennedy's campaign in 1960

• **Ottinger's Analogy.** Remember that a politician is like a contraceptive: He gives you a reasonable feeling of security while you are being screwed. *Ottinger's Law of the Executive Task.* When faced with a situation you "wouldn't touch with a ten-foot pole," your duty is to seek out a store selling eleven-foot poles.
—Charles Ottinger,
Mercerville, New Jersey

P

• **Parliament, Simple Rules for Interpreting Acts of.** Always avoid reading the preamble, which is likely to confuse rather than to enlighten. It sets forth not what the act is to do, but what it undoes, and confuses you with what the law was instead of telling you what it is to be.

When you come to a very long clause, skip it altogether, for it is sure to be unintelligible. If you try to attach one meaning to it, the lawyers are sure to attach another; and, therefore, if you are desirous of obeying an act of Parliament, it will be safer not to look at it, but wait until a few contrary decisions have been come to, and then act upon the latest.

When any clause says either one thing or the other shall be right, you may be sure that both will be wrong.

—This comes from an old British *Comic Almanac* and appears in the anthology *Comic Almanac,* edited by Thomas Yoseloff, published by A. S. Barnes and Co., New York, 1963

• **Perot's Political Polemic.** What most politicians stand for is reelection. If you can organize the grass roots, you could probably get a law passed saying the world's square.

> —H. Ross Perot; from Nick
> Nass

• **Philanthropy, First Law of.** It is more blessed to give than to receive, and it's deductible.

> —*Wall Street Journal* editorial

• **Pole's Law.** Every American President makes his predecessor look good.

> —J. R. Pole in *New Republic*

• **Political Law of Nature.** To err is human; to blame it on the other party is politics.

> —From *The Light Touch*, edit-
> ed by Charles Preston, Rand
> McNally and Co., 1965

• **Political Leadership, The First Law of.** Find out where the people want to go, then hustle yourself around in front of them.

> —James J. Kilpatrick, in
> *Nation's Business,* January
> 1979

• **Politicians' Rules.** (1) When the polls are in your favor, flaunt them. (2) When the polls are overwhelmingly unfavorable, (a) ridicule and dismiss them or (b) stress the volatility of public opinion. (3) When the polls are slightly unfavorable, play for sympathy as a struggling underdog. (4) When too close to call, be surprised at your own strength.

>—Unknown origin; from Jack Womeldorf, Washington, D.C.

• **Politico's Law.** No one ever lost an election for a speech he didn't make.

>—Marshall L. Smith, Rockville, Maryland

• **Posner's Distinction.** Only tax-supported institutions are closed on a minor holiday.

>—George E. Posner, Berkeley, California

• **Prentice's Congressional Constant.** There are two periods when Congress does no business: one is before the holidays, and the other after.

>—American journalist and humorist George D. Prentice

• **Price's Law of Politics.** It's easier to be a liberal a long way from home.

—Don Price, dean of
Harvard's Graduate School of
Government, who discovered
this when working with foun-
dations that were more willing to undertake controver-
sial projects overseas than in
the United States

• **Puck's Revision.** Ignorance of the law does
not prevent the losing lawyer from collecting his
bill.

—*Puck* magazine

• **Puzo's Assertion.** A lawyer with his brief-
case can steal more than a thousand men with
guns.

—Mario Puzo in *The
Godfather*

Q

• **Quayle's Clarification.** Republicans understand the importance of the bondage between parents and children.

> —Dan Quayle, at a
> September 1988 rally in
> Springfield, Illinois; quoted
> in *The Wit and Wisdom of
> George Bush* by Ken Brady
> and Jeremy Solomon

R

- **Rakove's Laws of Politics.** (1) The amount of effort put into a campaign by a worker expands in proportion to the personal benefits that he will derive from his party's victory. (2) The citizen is influenced by principle in direct proportion to his distance from the political situation.

> —Milton Rakove of the University of Illinois, who first spelled them out in the *Virginia Quarterly Review,* Summer 1965

- **Raskin's Zero Law.** The more zeros found in the price tag for a government program, the less congressional scrutiny it will receive.

> —Marcus Raskin, Institute for Policy Studies, Washington, D.C.; collected by Barbara Raskin, novelist

- **Reagan's Razor.** Anything we do is in the national interest.

—Ronald Reagan, quoted in
Lou Cannon's column,
Washington Post, January 19,
1986. The President had
uttered the line the previous
July when asked whether
sending helicopters to Bolivia
for drug enforcement was in
the national interest.

• **Reagan's Warning to Future First Ladies.**
Never wear a ring on your right hand in a
receiving line. It's always a little old lady who
will squeeze so hard she'll bring you to your
knees.

—Nancy Reagan, quoted in
Newsweek, May 18, 1987

• **Red Tape Rule.** To some people, cutting
red tape means cutting horizontally.

—Unknown/Radio station
KOA Denver, August 25, 1989

• **Regan's Answer to the Question of How
Social Security Will Be Funded in Fifty
Years.** I don't care, I'll be dead by then.

—Treasury Secretary Donald
Regan, quoted in the
Washington Star, April 18,
1981

• **Reynolds's First Law of Politics.**
Politicians will act rationally only when all other
alternatives are exhausted.

> —John Reynolds, Jr., Sandy,
> Utah

• **Rogers's Collected Thoughts on Law and
Politics.** (1) Politics ain't worrying this country
one-tenth as much as parking spaces. (2) The
minute you read something you can't understand, you can be almost sure it was drawn up
by a lawyer. (3) We are always saying, "Let the
law take its course." But what we really mean is
"Let the law take *our* course." (4) I don't think
you can make a lawyer honest by an act of legislature. You've got to work on his conscience.
And his lack of conscience is what makes him a
lawyer.

> —Will Rogers (1879–1935)
> from various sources

• **Rosenblatt's Law.** A politician who doesn't
swear at all is either an impostor or under
indictment.

> —Roger Rosenblatt, from his
> columns for the *Washington
> Post*

• **Rudd's Discovery.** You know that any senator or congressman could go home and make

$300,000–$400,000, but they don't. Why? Because they can stay in Washington and make it there.

> —Hughes Rudd, *Los Angeles Times*, August 15, 1980; from Robert D. Specht

• **Rumsfeld's Rules** (a sampling). *On Serving the President:* Don't play President—you're not. Where possible, preserve the President's options—he will very likely need them. •Never say "The White House wants"—buildings don't "want." •Don't speak ill of your predecessors (or successors)—you did not walk in their shoes. •*On Keeping Your Bearings in the White House:* Keep your sense of humor about your position. •Remember the observation (attributed to General Joe Stilwell) that "the higher a monkey climbs, the more you see of his behind"—you will find that it has more than a touch of truth. •Don't begin to believe you are indispensable or infallible, and don't let the President, or others, think you are—you're not. •Don't forget that the fifty or so invitations you receive a week are sent not because those people are just dying to see you but because of the position you hold. If you don't believe me, ask one of your predecessors how fast they stop. •If you are lost— "Climb, conserve, and confess." (From the student flight manual, as I recall from my days as a student naval aviator.) *On Doing the Job in the White House:* Read and listen for what is missing. Many advisers—in and out of government—are quite capable of telling the President how to improve what has been proposed, or what's gone wrong. Few seem capable of sensing what isn't there. *On Serving in Government:* (1) When an idea is being pushed because it is "exciting," "new," or "innovative"—beware. An exciting, new, innovative idea can also be foolish. (2) If in doubt, don't. If in doubt, do what is right. (3) Your best question is often "Why?" *On Politics, the Congress, and the Press:* (1) You can't win unless you are on the ballot. (2) Politics is human beings. (3) Politics is addition, not subtraction. (4) When someone with a rural accent says, "I don't know anything about politics," zip up your pockets. (5) If you try to please everybody, somebody is not going to like it. (6) With the press, it is safest to assume that there is no "off the record."

> —Donald Rumsfeld, from the rules and observations he created and collected while at the Pentagon and White House. The rules here were excerpted from an article in the February 1977 *Washingtonian* titled "Rumsfeld's Rules."

• **Ryan's Gap.** The interval between the election of your best friend and his hiring of your worst enemy to be his administrative assistant. On the average, Ryan's Gap is thirty-seven hours and twelve minutes.

> —John L. Ryan, quoted in
> *Conservative Digest,* April
> 1981; from Joseph C.
> Goulden

S

• **St. Elsewhere's Definition of Justice.** In our society, justice is a process, not a result.

> —From the television series "St. Elsewhere" from; James D. Haviland, Halifax, Nova Scotia, Canada

• **Sandburg's Law of Presidential Policy.** If he [the President] opens any door of policy, he is sure to hear it should be opened wider, it should be closed entirely, or there should be a new door, or return to the door that was there before, or the original intention of the Founding Fathers was that a window is better than a door anyhow.

> —Carl Sandburg; from James E. Farmer, Indianapolis, Indiana

• **Sattinger's Laws of Politics.** (1) The individual American voter has an extraordinary ability to simultaneously hold mutually contradictory political opinions. (2) Every politician knows how to balance the federal budget in such a way as to do the least damage to his prospects for reelection. (3) Whenever an event of political or economic significance occurs, it is immediately interpreted by each citizen in such a manner as to reinforce all previously held prejudices.

> —Irvin J. Sattinger, Ann Arbor, Michigan, who submitted these to The Murphy Center in 1980. Sattinger is author of the immutable and oft-quoted **Sattinger's Law,** which tells us: "It works better if you plug it in."

• **Seymour's Beatitude of the Bureaucracy —on the treatment of Employee Complaints.** The first time you're a disgruntled employee. The second time you're a pain in the ass. The third time you're a nut.

> —John Seymour, Bayonne, New Jersey

• **Shaffer's Law.** The effectiveness of a politician varies in inverse proportion to his commitment to principle.

> —Reporter Sam Shaffer writing in *Newsweek*

• **Shaw's Law.** The government that robs Peter to pay Paul can always depend on the support of Paul.

> —George Bernard Shaw;
> from James E. Farmer,
> Indianapolis, Indiana

• **Sheehan's Law of Rational Government.** Using logic to deal with government is illogical; using illogic to deal with government is logical.

> —Raymond J. Sheehan,
> Springfield, Massachusetts

• **Simonson's Laws.** (1) When all other reasons fail, local government officials who want to undertake large public projects will justify such expenditures by saying, "This is needed for our economic development." (2) If a public project is undertaken to stimulate economic development, there is a better-than-even chance it will do just the opposite.

> —Lee Simonson, Lewiston,
> New York

• **Skole's Restatement of the Old Boston Election Guideline.** Vote for a rich guy. He doesn't have to steal as much.

> —Bob Skole, Stockholm,
> Sweden, and Boston,
> Massachusetts

• **Smith's Laws of Politics.** (1) A politician always abuses his own constituency and placates the opponent's. (2) The main beneficiaries of federal aid are those states that most oppose the principle.

—Bob Smith, Washington, D.C., founder, editor, and publisher of *The Privacy Journal*

• **Smith's Political Dictum.** When caught with your hand in the cookie jar, it's easy to explain to your enemies, but try to explain it to your friends.

—James R. Smith, Petoskey, Michigan (see *Callahan's Corollary*)

• **Smolik's Law.** A politician will always be there when he needs you.

—Richard C. Smolik, St. Louis, Missouri

• **Spencer's (Contradictory) Corollary to Nofziger's Law of Detail.** If a political candidate chooses to go into specifics on a program that affects a voter's self-interest, the voter gets interested. If the proposal involves money, he gets very interested.

—Stuart Spencer of President

Ford's PR staff, on Reagan's
proposed $90 billion cut in
the federal budget; from Vic
Gold's *P.R. as in President*

• **Stapley's Law.** Never ask a politician for a
short answer, because the politician will then
give a longer answer than if you had not been so
specific about its length.
—Nigel Stapley, Dyfed, Wales

• **Star's Observation of Justice.** Somebody
has kidnapped justice and hidden it in the law.
—From the movie *The Star
Chamber;* submitted by James
D. Haviland, Halifax, Nova
Scotia, Canada

• **The Stark Theorem on Lobbyists.** The
more boring and incomprehensible a piece of
legislation is and the fewer taxpayers it affects,
the more lobbyists it will attract.
Or,

$$L(3) = \frac{P}{I} [AF^2 \times D] - 93(AFDC + SSI + \text{food stamps})$$

(*L*(3), the Length of a Line of Lobbyists,
equals the Population of the Nation (*P*) divided

by the Number of Individuals Impacted (*I*).
This figure is then multiplied by the square of
Arcaneness Factor (*AF*) times the Dullness
Factor (*D*) minus 93 times the number of refer-
ences to poor people.

> —Representative Pete Stark,
> California, whose findings
> were reported in *Washington
> Weekly,* October 22, 1984.
> The inspiration for this theo-
> rem was the scant turnout of
> lobbyists for Medicare hear-
> ings (affecting 26,758,000
> people), contrasted with the
> hordes who lobby for lower
> corporate taxes.

• **Steese's Law of the Body Politic.** It is
much more diffucult to discern the forest when
you're one of the trees.

> —Gerald Lee Steese, Long
> Beach, California

• **Stevenson's Presidential Paradox.** By the
time a man is nominated for the presidency of
the United States, he is no longer worthy to hold
the office.

> —Adlai Stevenson, 1956;
> from Sydney J. Harris

- **Stewart's Observation.** Believing is seeing.
  —John O. Stewart, Denver, Colorado, who explains, "The above was first appreciated as a result of interviewing many witnesses during the conduct of criminal investigations, but since then it has been found to account for much of what people perceive in any activity."

- **Straus's Axioms.** (1) Everything the government touches turns to solid waste. (2) After the government turns something to solid waste, it deregulates it and turns it into natural gas.
  —V. Michael Straus, Washington, D.C.

- **Strout's Law.** There is a major scandal in American political life every fifty years: Grant's in 1873, Teapot Dome in 1923, Watergate in 1973. Nail down your seats for 2023.
  —Richard Strout, *New Republic* columnist, quoted in *Time*, March 27, 1978

- **Survival Formula for Public Office.** (1) Exploit the inevitable (which means take credit for anything good that happens whether you had anything to do with it or not). (2) Don't disturb the perimeter (meaning, don't stir a mess unless you can be sure of the result). (3) Stay in with the Outs (the Ins will make so many mistakes you can't affort to alienate the Outs). (4) Don't permit yourself to get between a dog and a lamppost.

—Alan L. Otten

• **Szymanski's Inheritance Law.** Having been a physics major at the University of Notre Dame, having studied under one of Einstein's students, having worked on the Manhattan Project in World War II developing the atom bomb, and having been a physics teacher at the University of San Francisco, I thought I understood the Theory of Relativity. However, it wasn't until I became a probate judge that I really understood the Theory. It is that, at death, you have a number of relatives directly proportionate to the amount of money you leave behind.

—The late Judge Frank S. Szymanski from his son David J. Szymanski, Judge of Probate, Wayne County, Michigan

T

- **Thatcher's Law of Politics.** The unexpected happens.

> —Revealed by former British Prime Minister Margaret Thatcher at the National Press Club, Washington, D.C., June 26, 1995

- **Thermodynamics of Political Gossip.** When affection for a sitting President cools down, the chatter about the senior available Kennedy heats up.

> —*Newsweek,* May 8, 1978

- **Tiberius's Law of Politicians.** Caesar doesn't want Caesar's. Caesar wants God's.

> —N. Sally Hass, Sleepy Hollow, Illinois. Named for the vicious Tiberius Claudius Nero Caesar.

- **Todd's Laws.** Emotion is a rotten base for politics.

> —Uttered by a character in

Dick Francis's *In the Farm,*
1976; from Charles D. Poe

• **Trace's Law.** Whenever a political body
passes legislation on behalf of the consumer, the
consumer will wait longer and pay more for the
same product or service.
>—Richard W. Trace,
>Kingston, Michigan

• **TRB's Law of Scandals.** When wrongdo-
ing is exposed, the real scandal is what's legal.
>—Timothy Noah, *New
>Republic,* July 11, 1988. TRB
>is a long-established pseudo-
>nym for the opinion colum-
>nist in the magazine.

• **Truman's Advice for Politicians Moving
to Washington.** If you really want a friend in
this town, get yourself a dog.
>—President Harry S Truman.
>When this was quoted to a
>newly elected President Bill
>Clinton, he responded, "I
>wish someone had told me
>that before I showed up with
>a neutered cat."

• **Truman's Law of Qualifications.** Always vote for the better man. He is a Democrat. Anyone who votes for a Republican gets what he deserves.

—Harry S Truman

• **Tufte's First Law of Political Economy.** The politicians who make economic policy operate under conditions of political competition.

—Edward R. Tufte, professor of political science, Yale University, from his *Political Control of the Economy;* submitted by Theodore C. Achilles

U

• **Udall's Fourth Law of Politics.** If you can find something everyone agrees on, it's wrong.
—Morris Udall, quoted in the
New York Times, April 4, 1975

• **Unintended Consequences, Law of.** Government regulations always have unintended consequences, and their importance outweighs the intended consequences.
—Created in the mid-1930s by Columbia University sociologist Robert K. Merton, it is commonly cited, for instance, when trying to explain why the movement to create rights for the mentally ill through deinstitutionalization created so many homeless people.

• **Unruh's Understanding of Political Alliances.** If I had slain all my enemies yesterday, I wouldn't have any friends today.

>—The late Jesse Unruh, California state treasurer; from Tom Gill. Unruh also uttered one of the most quoted lines of his time: "Money is the mother's milk of politics."

V

• **Valenti's Rule for a Successful Political Career.** Do your own xeroxing.

> —Attributed to Jack Valenti when he was an adviser to Lyndon B. Johnson, but more recently expanded to include paper shredding

• **Veeck's Distinction.** Next to the confrontation between two highly trained, finely honed batteries of lawyers, jungle warfare is a finely tuned minuet.

> —Baseball maverick Bill Veeck in *The Hustler's Handbook*, Berkley Books (1965)

• **Vidal's Conclusion.** For certain people, after fifty, litigation takes the place of sex.

> —Author Gore Vidal, quoted in the *Evening Standard*, 1981

W

- **Walinsky's Law of Political Campaigns.** If there are twelve clowns in a ring, you can jump in the middle and start reciting Shakespeare, but to the audience, you'll just be the thirteenth clown.

> —Adam Walinsky, quoted by Alan Otten in the *Wall Street Journal*

- **Washington's First Law of Summer.** Because so little of consequence happens here in August, whatever does occur is embellished, embroidered, and otherwise exaggerated far beyond reality.

> —Political writer Robert Walters, who used the law to explain *l'affaire* Andrew Young during the summer of 1979 (Young had, as the United States' U.N. delegate, met unofficially with members of the Palestine Liberation Organization)

• **The Washington Rule.** No one is ever to be held accountable for anything done in the course of business. *Corollary:* In official Washington, you can try to murder a foreign leader by day and make small talk with his ambassador that evening.

> —Columnist Richard Cohen, *Washington Post,* January 14, 1986

• **Washington's Seven Cardinal Rules.**
(1) Don't make enemies you don't need to make.
(2) Don't start believing you're indispensable.
(3) Don't confuse what's good for you with what's good for the President. (4) Don't forget that you are not the elected official. (5) Don't start blaming the boss if you get into trouble. (6) Don't unilaterally announce you are going to run things, rather than letting the President announce who will run things. (7) Someone must pay the price when the polls plummet, and anyone who has maintained a high profile will be a prime target.

> —Maureen Dowd in an article titled "Sununu Downfall: He Broke 7 Cardinal Rules," *New York Times,* December 5, 1991

• **West's Rules.** *Legislation:* The more pork in the barrel, the faster it rolls. *Cash Flow:* If he can shut off your water, pay him first.
>—Roy West, Philadelphia, Pennsylvania

• **Whatley's Proliferation.** Fat is hereditary —you get it from your government.
>—Craig Whatley, San Rafael, California

• **White House, First Law of Life in the.** Don't do anything you're not prepared to see in the papers the next morning.
>—Stated by a former White House staffer at the time of the Dr. Peter Bourne resignation; quoted in *Newsweek*, July 31, 1978

• **White's National Security Rule.** Security declines as security machinery expands.
>—E. B. White, quoted in *Federal Times*, October 29, 1979; from Joseph C. Goulden

• **White's Political Rule of Thumb.** Political campaigns do not truly start until the guys in bars stop arguing about the World Series.

> —Teddy White, quoted in
> *National Review,* July 8, 1988;
> from Charles D. Poe

• **Will's Rule of Informed Citizenship.** If you want to understand your government, don't begin by reading the Constitution. (It conveys precious little of the flavor of today's statecraft.) Instead read selected portions of the Washington telephone directory containing listings for all the organizations with titles beginning with the word "National."

> —George Will; from Jack
> Womeldorf

• **Williams's Discovery.** You get to go on a guy's front lawn and kick him in the shorts every night.

> —NBC's Brian Williams, on
> why being a White House
> correspondent is a fun job;
> quoted in *The Hill,* August 16,
> 1995

• **Williams's Law of Political Rhetoric.** Never underestimate the ability of a politician to (a) say something and not tell you very much,

(b) do it with style, and (c) touch all the bases.
> —Robert H. Williams, in the
> *Washington Post*. His proof
> was a statement made by
> Senator Henry M. "Scoop"
> Jackson to Israel's Prime
> Minister Menachem Begin:
> "As we Christians approach
> the Christmas season, we can
> all be thankful to a Moslem
> and a Jew."

• **The Willis Catch-88.** No matter who he is, the next President of the United States will be perceived to be a failure, because his duties have been multiplied dramatically, while his hands will be tied by a crippling national debt and deficit, and by a Congress that is oversensitive to the "wish lists" of single-issue pressure groups, including ex-congressmen turned professional lobbyists.
> —Jane B. Willis, letter to the
> *Sarasota Herald-Tribune,* April
> 15, 1988; from Ben Willis, Jr.

• **Wolfe's Law.** In this world you get laws; in the next you get justice.
> —Unknown caller named
> Wolfe on radio station KOA
> in Denver, Colorado

• **Wolpe's Law of Political Survival.** Why
lose today if you can lose tomorrow?
> —Public affairs consultant
> Bruce C. Wolpe, North
> Sydney, Australia

_X-Y-Z_

• **Yakovlev's Rule of Diplomacy.** Everyone is entitled to say "no"—except diplomats.

>   —Aleksandr Yakovlev, Soviet
>   Politburo member and chief
>   architect of Mikhail
>   Gorbachev's _glasnost_ policy,
>   from an interview in the
>   _Washington Times,_ December
>   9, 1988; from Joseph C.
>   Goulden

— *Special Bonus Sections* —

How to Tell the Difference between Democrats and Republicans

Most of these distinctions are from documents published in the *Congressional Record*, and were submitted by Representative Craig Hosmer (R-California) and Andrew Jacobs, Jr. (D-Indiana) in 1974 and 1983 respectively. Both said that the authors chose to remain anonymous. These are, in fact, recent embellishments of lists telling of the party differences dating back much earlier. In his autobiography, David Brinkley talks about hundreds of variations on the theme. Brinkley's favorite was a set inserted in the *Congressional Record* in 1956 by Will Stanton that includes some of the same distinctions used by Hosmer and Jacobs. The rest are attributed to various sources but mostly come from a series of 1994 columns by Bob Levey in the *Washington Post* in which readers were asked to send in their pet distinctions.

• Democrats buy most of the books that have been banned somewhere. Republicans form censorship committees and read them as a group.

• Republicans consume three-fourths of all the rutabagas produced in this country. The remainder is thrown out.

• Republicans employ exterminators. Democrats step on the bugs.

• Democrats believe people are basically good but must be saved from themselves by their government. Republicans believe people are basically bad but they'll be okay if they're left alone. (Andy Rooney, from *A Few Minutes with Andy Rooney*)

• Democrats name their children after currently popular sports figures, politicians, and entertainers. Republican children are named after their parents or grandparents, according to where the money is.

• On Saturday, Republicans head for the hunting lodge or the yacht club. Democrats wash the car and get a haircut.

• Republicans smoke cigars on weekdays.

• Republicans eat escargot. Democrats eat snails. (Kevin Mellema of Falls Church, Virginia)

• Republicans have guest rooms. Democrats have spare rooms filled with old baby furniture.

• Democrats suffer from chapped hands and headaches. Republicans have tennis elbow and gout.

• Democrats leave the dishes in the drying rack on the sink overnight. Republicans put the dishes away every night. (Andy Rooney, from *A Few Minutes with Andy Rooney*)

• Democrats keep trying to cut down on smoking but are not successful. Neither are Republicans.

• Republicans think skid row is a disgrace. Democrats think it merely needs a $530 million grant from HUD. (Martha Watson of Washington, D.C.)

• Republicans tend to keep their shades drawn, although there is seldom any reason why they should. Democrats ought to, but don't.

• Republicans study the financial pages of the newspaper. Democrats put them in the bottom of the birdcage.

• Most of the stuff alongside the road has been thrown out of car windows by Democrats.

• When the attendant brings the car up from an underground parking lot, Republicans walk all the way around it and check for nicks and chips. Democrats don't bother, because they're so relieved that the car wasn't stolen. (Eric Grimm of Washington, D.C.)

• Republicans raise dahlias, dalmations, and eyebrows. Democrats raise Airedales, kids, and taxes.

• As children, Democrats played Spin the Bottle and Pin the Tail on the Donkey. Republicans played Monopoly. (Nancy L. Peters of Arlington, Virginia)

• Democrats eat the fish they catch. Republicans hang them on the wall.

• Democrats eat soybeans. Republicans' livestock eat soybeans. (Andrew C. Spitzler, of Silver Spring, Maryland)

• Republican boys date Democratic girls. They plan to marry Republican girls, but feel they're entitled to a little fun first.

• Large cities such as New York are filled with Republicans up until 5 P.M. At this point people begin pouring out of every exit of the city. These are Republicans going home.

• Democrats make up plans and then do something else. Republicans follow the plans their grandfathers made.

• Republicans are the victims of restructuring. Democrats get laid off. (Roland Williams of Burke, Virginia)

• Republicans sleep in twin beds—some even in separate rooms. That is why there are more Democrats.

• Republicans think that they are holier than thou. Democrats know that they are. (Frank N. Grateau of Charlottesville, Virginia)

• Democrats love television and watch a lot of it. Republicans hate television. They watch a lot of it, too. (Andy Rooney, from *A Few Minutes with Andy Rooney*)

• Democrats give their worn-out clothes to those less fortunate. Republicans wear theirs.

(John E. Fagan of Washington, D.C.)

- Democrats see the water glass as half empty. Republicans want to know who the hell drank their water. (Gordon Thomas of Arlington, Virginia)

- Republicans touch up the paint on their bumpers to maintain the resale value of their cars. Democrats are trying to figure out how to rip CLINTON/GORE stickers off theirs (Marshall Goode of Sterling, Virginia)

- Democrats think heavy metal is a kind of rock-and-roll. Republicans think it's an investment opportunity. (Arthur Weitz of Bethesda, Maryland)

- Democrats call "finding their inner self" what Republicans call a "midlife crisis." (Eileen Burke of Washington, D.C., and Christine Basso of Allentown, Pennsylvania)

- Republicans do what's right, Democrats do what's fair; but if either wants a tax reduction, both are doomed. (Joe, a radio call-in guest on WIND, Chicago)

- Finally, there is mega-distinction: Foreigners often ask what the difference is between American political parties. It is really very simple. With the Republicans, you worry that they have not found solutions to the nation's problems. With the Democrats, you are afraid that they might think of something. (H. Coucheron-Aamot of Albuquerque, New Mexico)

How to Differentiate Liberals from Conservatives

This is primarily the work of N. Sally Hass, Sleepy Hollow, Illinois. She developed this scale when she discovered, "Many people think that liberals are permissive and conservatives are strict. Not so. Liberals are both permissive and strict, as are conservatives, but they are permissive and strict about different things." A few additions have been made to the original and re-ordered Hass list; they are properly attributed.

(1) Liberals want to continue the ban on prayer in the public schools, as they consider religion to be personal and private. They favor compulsory sex education. Conservatives want to ban sex education. They favor compulsory prayer.

(2) Conservatives want to outlaw pornography. Liberals want to outlaw handguns.

(3) Liberals want to solve the marijuana problem by making it legal. Conservatives want to solve the wife-beating problem by making it legal.

(4) Liberals want to strike down the abortion laws, so that unwanted babies can be killed off before they are born. Conservatives want to strike down the welfare laws, so that unwanted

babies can be starved to death after they are born.

(5) The conservative would prevent rape by locking up his wife and daughters. The liberal would prevent rape by legalizing prostitution. Neither considers locking up rapists, because the liberal says it is society's fault and the conservative says it costs too much money.

(6) A conservative sees a man drowning fifty feet from shore, throws him a twenty-five-foot-long rope, and tells him to swim to it. A liberal throws him a rope fifty feet long, then drops his end and goes off to perform another good deed.

(7) Conservatives curb their dogs. Liberals keep cats and curb other people's dogs.

(8) Conservatives call it nuclear war and liberals call it thermonuclear war. (Charles D. Poe)

(9) When it comes to equal rights for women, the conservative doesn't want to monkey with the Constitution. When it comes to a balanced federal budget, the liberal doesn't want to monkey with the Constitution. (Unknown origin, submitted by the late Theodore C. Achilles, Washington, D.C.)

Glossary of Legal Terms

(Collected from a variety of sources. All those that cannot be attributed belong to that skilled contributor to all anthologies: Anon.)

Appeal. When you ask one court to show its contempt for another court. (Finley Peter Dunn)

"As Your Honor Well Recalls . . ." Tip-off by a lawyer that he is about to refer to a long-forgotten or imaginary case. (Adapted from a similar definition by Miles Kington, *Punch*, November 12, 1975)

Basic Concept. Murder—don't do it; theft—don't do it; fraud—don't do it; etc. (G. Guy Smith, Media, Pennsylvania)

Bench Warrant. A guaranteed seat in court. (D. Robert White's *The Official Lawyer's Handbook*)

Brief. Long and windy document. Should be at least 10,000 words long to qualify. (Anon.)

Costs. Amount required to bankrupt the acquitted. (Miles Kington)

Courtroom. A place where Jesus Christ and Judas Iscariot would be equals, with the betting odds in favor of Judas. (H. L. Mencken)

Duty of the Lawyer. When there is a rift in the lute, the business of the lawyer is to widen the rift and gather the loot. (Arthur Garfield Hays)

Ex Lax. Latin, "From the lawyer." Refers to memos, briefs, and other work products of lawyers. (D. Robert White's *The Official Lawyer's Handbook*)

Habeus Corpus. 1. A writ by which a man may be taken out of jail when confined for the wrong crime. (Ambrose Bierce). 2. Latin, "You've got a body." A conversation opener at discotheques in ancient Rome. (D. Robert White's *The Official Lawyer's Handbook*)

Incongruous. Where our laws are made. (Bennett Cerf)

"It has been long known that . . ." "I haven't been able to find the original reference."

"It might be argued that . . ." "I have such a good answer for this argument that I want to make sure it is raised."

Jail. Where they keep the litter of the law. (Leonard Louis Levinson)

Jury. Twelve persons chosen to decide who has the better lawyer. (Robert Frost, attributed)

Justice. A commodity that in a more or less adulterated state the State sells to its citizens as a reward for their allegiance, taxes, and personal service.

Lawful. Compatible with the will of the judge having jurisdiction. (Ambrose Bierce)

Lawsuit. A successful lawsuit is one worn by a politician. (Robert Frost)

Lawyer. 1. One skilled in the circumvention of the law. (Ambrose Bierce) 2. A man who makes his living by the sweat of his browbeating. (James Huneker) 3. One who protects us against robbers by taking away the temptation. (H. L. Mencken, *Sententiae*)

Lawyers. The only persons in whom ignorance of the law is not punished. (Jeremy Bentham)

Lex Clio Volente. The client is always right—particularly when he has further causes to entrust. (Del Goldsmith, *American Bar Association Journal*)

Litigant. A person about to give up his skin for the hope of saving his bones. (Ambrose Bierce)

Nine Points of the Law, the. (1) A good deal of money. (2) A good deal of patience. (3) A good case. (4) A good lawyer. (5) A good counsel. (6) Good witnesses. (7) A good jury. (8) A good judge. (9) Good luck.

Oath. In law, a solemn appeal to the Deity, made binding upon the conscience by a penalty for perjury. (Ambrose Bierce)

Obscenity. Whatever gives a judge an erection. (Anonymous lawyer in Jonathon Green's *Cynic's Lexicon*)

Philadelphia Lawyer. An heir-splitter.
(Leonard Louis Levinson)

Plea Bargaining. Ending a sentence with a proposition.

Proper Pronoun. Louis Nizer has pointed out that most lawyers, on winning a case, will say, "We have won," but when justice frowns on the case the lawyer customarily remarks, "You have lost."

Res Ipsa Loquitur. Latin for "the thing speaks for itself." Anything that speaks for itself is an abomination to the law and reason enough for a lawyer to be paid to speak for something that speaks for itself. (Adapted from Miles Kington)

Settlement. A device by which lawyers obtain fees without working for them.
(D. Robert White's *The Official Lawyer's Handbook*)

Will. Where there's a will, there's a lawsuit. (Oliver Herford)

"With All Due Respect . . ." Introductory phrase for a disrespectful statement.

"Yes, Your Honor." Witty rejoinder by lawyer to judge. (Miles Kington)

Afterwords

This is the third work in a series of books that are intended to help describe elements of the real world through laws, rules, principles, and maxims.

Needless to say, I as the Director of The Murphy Center am ever eager to collect new laws and hear from readers. Write to me in care of:

The Murphy Center
Box 80
Garrett Park, MD 20896-0080

The Center sees itself as a research institution that is unique in the sense that it refuses federal funding, foundation grants, and any other attempt to subvert its cynical independence with cash. It is at work on a number of key research issues, including that of trying to find a loophole in the universal law that says "There is no such thing as a free lunch."

One of the benefits that accrue to those who help The Murphy Center with its research is their appointment as fellows of The Murphy Center. The value of such a title should be reckoned by the fact that it can be given only by the Director and cannot be bought (at least not cheaply) and cannot be taken away by anyone but the Director (who has yet to decommission a Fellow). There are now so many Fellows that it would be impossible to list all of them—as was the practice in earlier Center publications.

There is, however, a select group of people who have contributed so much to the work of the Center over the past twenty years that they have achieved the rank of Senior Fellow. They cannot be thanked enough, but I will do it one more time: the late Theodore C. Achilles, Joseph E. Badger, Nancy Dickson, the late Russell Dunn Sr., Fred Dyer, M. Mack Earle, John Ehrman, Tom Gill, Joseph C. Goulden, Shel Kagan, Edward Logg, Martin Kottmeyer, Herbert H. Paper, the late Charles D. Poe, Frank S. Preston, Conrad Schneiker, Bob and Monika Skole, Marshall L. Smith, Robert D. Specht, Steve Stine, Gregg Townsend, Neal Wilgus, Bennett Willis Jr., Jack Womeldorf, Steve Woodbury, and Donald R. Woods.

Index

PAUL DICKSON

Corruption. Acton's, The Cook County Immutable Law
Cost-effectiveness. Brooks's (3)

Debate. Abourezk's, Hegel's, Knowles's
Deception. Maverick's, McAdoo's, Moynihan's
Defense. Lament for Public Defenders
Democracy. Chaplin's, Davidson's, Greenfield's (2), Jacquin's, Kelleher's, Murray's Rule
Democrats. Greenfield's (1), Truman's Law,
    How to Tell the Difference Between Republicans and (Special Bonus Sections)
Details. Nofziger's, Spencer's
Diplomacy. Cradock's, Yakovlev's
Disasters. Drake's
Discovery. Adams's, Babbitt's, Barnicle's, Bush's, Crenna's, Enthoven's, Honig's, Kissinger's, Rudd's, Williams's Discovery
Distinction. Anderson's, Veeck's
Divorce. Beste's (7)
Document/Documentation. Bierman's

Economics. Ackley's, Baer's, Simonson's, Tufte's,
Elections. Bendiner's, Dirksen's, Politico's, Skole's
Emotion. Todd's

Endorsements. Baker's Secrets (10)
Enemies. Abourezk's, Cruickshank's, Curley's, Smith's Political Dictum, Unruh's, Washington's (1)
Energy. Brooks's
Environment. Brooks's
Equality. France's
Equations. Giller's,
Errors. Moriarty's (2)
Evolution. Babbitt's
Executives. Ottinger's
Expenses. Beck's (2), Guppy Law
Explanation. Cotton's, Kelleher's

Facts. Adams's, Beck's (4), Mills's
Favors. Alinsky's
Federal Funds/Grants. Baker's First Law, Smith's Laws (2)
First Ladies. Reagan's Warning
Friendship. Evans's, Ryan's, Smith's Political Dictum, Truman's Advice, Unruh's
Future. Crenna's

Geometry. Baker's First Law
Gossip. Thermodynamics of Political Gossip
Government. Armey's (2), Brooks's, Cruickshank's, Drake's, Frankel's ,Raskin's, Rumsfeld's, Shaw's, Sheehan's, Straus's, Whatley's, Will's
Governors. Baker's First

118

Theorem, Kenworthy's, The
Stark Theorem
Logic. Sheehan's
Loss/Lost. Wolpe's
Loyalty. Baker's Secret (3)
Lunch. Niebuhr's

Media. Beck's (1)
Memoranda. Acheson's
Memory. Cohen's
Money. Dart's, Flory's,
Keynes's, McAdoo's,
Raskin's, Regan's, Rudd's,
Spencer's, Szymanski's,
Unruh's, West's
Mottos. Boren's

National Interest. Reagan's
Razor
National Security. White's
National Security Rule
Nation's Capital. Broder's
(2), Dean's
Negotiation. Chuck's

Opinions. Sattinger's (1)
Opponents. Baker's Secret
(7,8)
Oratory. Alsop's, Muskie's

**Parliament/Parliamentary
Procedure.** Parliament,
Simple Rules for
Patriotism. Chesterton's
Permanence. Cohen's
Personal Relations. Cotton's
Philanthropy. Philanthropy,
First Law of
Photocopiers. Beste's (5)
Policy. McClaughry's,
Sandburg's

Politicians. Anderson's,
Baker's Secrets (2), Beck's
(1), Bendiner's, Dart's,
Davis's, DeRoy's, Fannie's,
Foley's, Hall's (2), Herold's,
Kilpatrick's, Lippman's,
Lloyd George's,
Mankiewicz's, Mann's,
Mitchell's, Naiman's,
Ottinger's, Perot's,
Politicians', Reynolds's,
Rosenblatt's, Sattinger's (2),
Shaffer's, Smith's (1),
Smith's Political Dictum,
Smolik's, Stapley's,
Tiberius's, Tufte's, William's
Law
Politics. Anderson's,
Abourezk's, Adams's,
Anderson's, Armey's, Baer's,
Baker's Secrets (5), Beck's
(3), Byrd's, Callahan's,
Clinton's Law, Clinton's
Rules, Cohen's, The Cook
County Immutable Law,
Curley's, Dirksen's, Dugger's,
Landon's, McCarthy's Law,
O'Brien's, Political Law of
Nature, Rakove's, Rogers's
(1), Rumsfeld's, Survival
Formula, Thatcher's, Todd's,
Udall's, Valenti's
Polls. Cohen's, Politicians',
Washington's Seven
Cardinal Rules (7)
Pork. Enthoven's
Potholes. Byrd's
Power. Acton's, Cohen's,
Evans's, Maddocks's
Prayer. Miles's
Predecessors. Ackley's, Pole's